MANTISES

MANTISES

by Sylvia A. Johnson

Photographs by Satoshi Kuribayashi

A Lerner Natural Science Book

Lerner Publications Company • Minneapolis

Sylvia A. Johnson, Series Editor

Translation of original text by Kay Kushino

Photographs on pages 7 and 34 by Yuko Sato

*The publisher wishes to thank Jerry W. Heaps,
Department of Entomology, University of Minnesota,
for his assistance in the preparation of this book.*

The glossary on page 46 gives definitions and pronunciations
of words shown in **bold type** in the text.

LIBRARY OF CONGRESS CATALOGING IN PUBLICATION DATA

Johnson, Sylvia A.
    Mantises.

    (A Lerner natural science book)
    Adaptation of: Kamakiri no kansatsu / by Satoshi Kuribayashi.
    Includes index.
    Summary: Describes the habits and life cycle of mantises, in-
cluding the hatching of eggs, development of young, and final molt
that produces adult insects.
    1. Praying mantis—Juvenile literature. [1. Praying mantis]
I. Kuribayashi, Satoshi, 1939-   ill. II. Kuribayashi, Satoshi,
1939-   . Kamakiri no himitsu. III. Title. IV. Series.
QL508.M2J58 1984   595.7'25   83-23889
ISBN 0-8225-1458-3 (lib. bdg.)

This edition first published 1984 by Lerner Publications Company.
Text copyright © 1984 by Lerner Publications Company.
Photographs copyright © 1976 by Satoshi Kuribayashi.
Text adapted from OBSERVING MANTISES © 1976 by Satoshi Kuribayashi.
English language rights arranged by Kurita-Bando Literary Agency
for Akane Shobo Publishers, Tokyo, Japan.

International Standard Book Number: 0-8225-1458-3
Library of Congress Catalog Card Number: 83-23889

    3   4   5   6   7   8   9   10   93   92   91   90   89   88   87   86   85

The insect has a long, graceful body and a small, heart-shaped head. When it is at rest, it looks like a person with arms raised in devout prayer. When it moves, it moves with lightning speed, and the praying "arms" become fierce weapons that grip and tear.

What kind of creature is this that looks so elegant and serene and yet attacks with such deadly force? It is a mantis, one of the most unusual and fascinating members of the insect tribe.

Here are 2 of the more than 1,500 species of mantises. Shown above is the Chinese mantis *(Tenodera aridifolia),* which was imported to North America in the 1890s. Most of the insects shown in this book are Chinese mantises.

This curious insect, the mantis, can be found in many parts of the world with temperate or tropical climates. There are at least 1,500 different **species,** or kinds, of mantises, ranging from small insects less than ½ inch (12.5 millimeters) long to giants measuring over 6 inches (150 millimeters).

Although mantises are fairly common insects, there are many things that scientists do not know about them. One unanswered question about mantises has to do with their place in the world of insects. What insect group do they belong to, and who are their closest relatives?

Grasshoppers (left) and crickets (right) are close relatives of the mantis.

Most scientists agree that mantises are related to grasshoppers, crickets, cockroaches, and other members of the order **Orthoptera**. Like these insects, mantises have mouthparts designed to chew food. They also have distinctive wings, the front pair usually thick and narrow, and the back pair thin and folded like a fan.

Because mantises share these and other characteristics with Orthopteran insects, they are often considered members of this order. Some scientists believe, however, that mantises are different enough from grasshoppers, crickets, and cockroaches to be given their own order, **Mantodea**.

Let's take a closer look at mantises to discover how unusual these insects really are.

A mantis egg case attached to a tree

If you live in an area with a temperate climate, spring is the best time of year to begin observing mantises. In early spring, before the new leaves have appeared on the

Above: Mantis eggs inside an egg case. *Right:* As the spring weather becomes warmer, the eggs begin to develop into young mantises.

trees, you can go out into the woods and fields and look for the **egg cases** from which new mantises will soon emerge.

These egg cases, which scientists call **oothecae**, were made by female mantises during the previous autumn. They are constructed of a spongy material with a hard outer surface. Attached to twigs and branches, the cases have survived the long, cold winter, concealing within their hard shells the eggs laid by the females. Now as the spring days become warmer, the eggs begin to develop into young mantises.

By May or June, the baby mantises have completed their development and are ready to emerge into the outside world.

Left: Young mantises emerging from an egg case. *Opposite:* The mantises remain attached to the case by silk threads produced in their abdomens.

To escape from the egg case, the young mantises must wiggle through narrow passages leading to openings in the outside of the case. As each mantis comes out head first from an opening, it remains attached to the case by means of two fine silk threads produced from a gland in its abdomen.

When a young mantis first emerges, it looks something like a tiny worm with large, dark eyes. It is enclosed in a thin, transparent membrane that holds its long legs tight against its body.

There may be as many as 400 young mantises inside a single egg case. As more and more youngsters push their way out through the openings, they form a living stream of wriggling, twisting bodies.

10

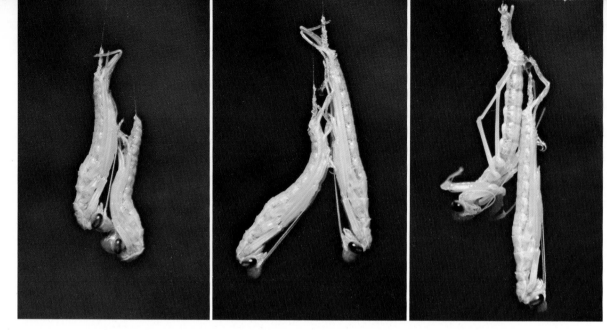

Left and center: Dangling from their silk threads, these two young mantises are struggling to escape from the membranes that enclose them. *Right:* After 30 seconds of hard work, the mantis on the left has almost completed the job.

After emerging from the egg case, a young mantis must free itself from its enclosing membrane before it can do anything else. It performs this escape act while dangling head down from its silk threads. Moving and twisting its body, it finally breaks through the membrane and frees its legs.

As soon as the mantis is able to move freely, it begins to scramble up the string to the egg case. From here, it will try to reach a branch of a nearby tree or bush. At the same time, all the other emerging youngsters are breaking through their membranes and scrambling for freedom. The little mantises climb and crawl over each other in their haste to escape from the place of their birth.

Above: Both mantises rest after freeing themselves from their membranes. *Right:* The mantis on the left begins to climb back up the silk thread toward the egg case.

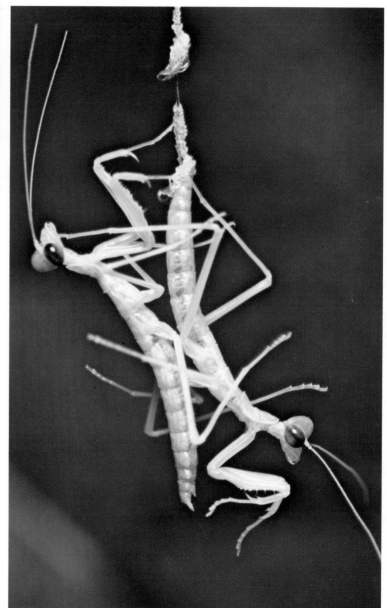

13

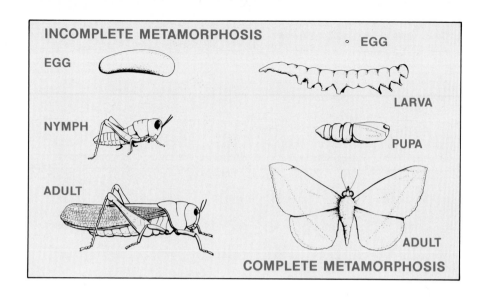

INCOMPLETE METAMORPHOSIS

EGG

NYMPH

ADULT

EGG

LARVA

PUPA

ADULT

COMPLETE METAMORPHOSIS

After a young mantis has escaped from the confining membrane, its resemblance to an adult mantis is easier to see. In fact, an immature mantis, or **nymph,** is very similar to its parents except that it is much smaller and has no wings. As the nymph grows, it will become larger and develop wings just like those of an adult mantis.

The development of a mantis from egg to nymph to adult is the same as the development of grasshoppers, crickets, dragonflies, and a few other insects. This gradual pattern of growth is called **incomplete metamorphosis.** Butterflies, ants, bees, beetles, and many other kinds of insects go through a more complicated, four-stage development known as **complete metamorphosis.** In complete metamorphosis, the changes in appearance and habits that take place between the different stages are more extreme than the gradual development of incomplete metamorphosis.

15

Spiders (opposite), lizards (above right), and ants (below right) are among the animals that prey on mantis nymphs.

After a mantis nymph makes its escape from the egg case, it waits quietly in the trees or grass nearby. Its body is soft, and its pale color makes it easy to see. Until the nymph's body hardens and changes to a darker color, the little insect is very vulnerable to attack by **predators**.

Many kinds of animals are eager to make a meal of the newly emerged nymphs. Spiders as well as ants and other insects feed on the tiny mantises. Birds, lizards, frogs, and toads also find the nymphs to be easy **prey**. Many of the hundreds of nymphs that emerge from an egg case do not survive the first few hours of their lives.

With their pale coloring, young mantis nymphs stand out against the dark green leaves of a plant.

18

Left: A nymph makes a meal of an aphid. *Right:* This nymph is cleaning itself after eating.

If a mantis nymph survives the dangerous early period of its life, it soon develops a fierce appetite for food. Nymphs, like adult mantises, are strictly meat-eaters. Their diets are made up of the bodies of insects that they hunt and kill.

Many insects that go through complete metamorphosis eat different kinds of foods in the different stages of their lives. For instance, the larvae or caterpillars of most butterflies eat plant leaves, while the adult butterflies feed only on flower nectar or sometimes eat nothing at all.

Insects like mantises that develop through incomplete metamorphosis often keep the same eating habits throughout their lives. When a mantis nymph seizes its first insect and devours it, it is starting on a life-long career as a predator.

Opposite: A nymph going through its fourth molt. Its head has emerged, but its long antennae are still caught in the old exoskeleton. *Right:* The nymph rests after finishing its molt.

As a nymph becomes expert at finding nourishing food, its body begins to grow larger. Like all insects, a mantis nymph grows in a special way. In order to increase in size, it must replace the outer covering of its body.

An insect's body is enclosed in a tough, flexible covering called an **exoskeleton.** As the word suggests, this covering acts as an exterior skeleton, serving the same purpose as the bony, internal skeletons of other kinds of animals.

Unlike bones, however, an insect's exoskeleton does not grow along with its body. As the insect gets larger, its exoskeleton eventually becomes too tight. When this happens, the old exoskeleton is shed, or **molted,** and replaced by a new, roomier one that forms underneath it.

21

As a nymph gradually develops the green coloring of an adult mantis, it becomes difficult for predators to see.

A mantis nymph that has emerged in spring usually molts six or seven times during the summer months. With each successive molt, its exoskeleton gradually changes in color from creamy white to light brown to a leafy shade of green. This green coloring makes it easy for the nymph to blend in with its environment and conceal itself from predators.

Another change that takes place during the nymph's molts is the gradual development of the insect's wings. After the first molt, the two pairs of wings appear as tiny pads on the back of the nymph's **thorax,** the middle section of its body. The **wing pads** grow with each molt, but they will not be completely developed until the nymph goes through the final molt and emerges as an adult insect.

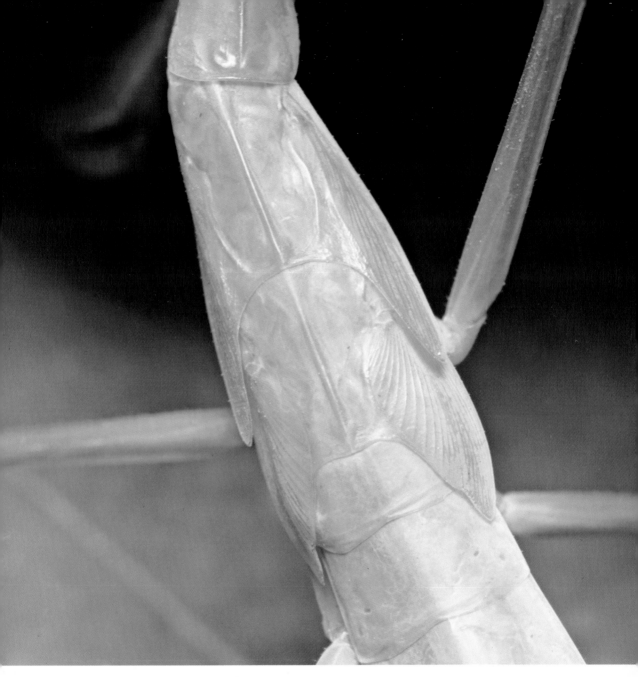

This nymph has already molted six times. Its developing wings can be seen clearly on its thorax.

Left: A nymph about to begin its final molt. *Opposite:* These photographs show the various stages in the final molt that produces an adult mantis.

A nymph's final molt (shown in the pictures on the opposite page) usually occurs in late summer or early autumn. It takes place like all the other molts, with the nymph hanging head down from a twig or branch. The old exoskeleton splits down the back, and the insect begins to pull the front part of its body out (1). By using a series of jerking movements, it eventually frees all six legs (2) and then its entire body (3) from the discarded exoskeleton.

Clinging to the branch with its front legs, the mantis gradually expands its long wings (4 and 5). The wings and body are soft and pale in color, but they gradually harden and become darker as the mantis perches quietly on its branch (6).

About a day after its final molt is completed, the mantis is fully developed and ready to begin its adult life.

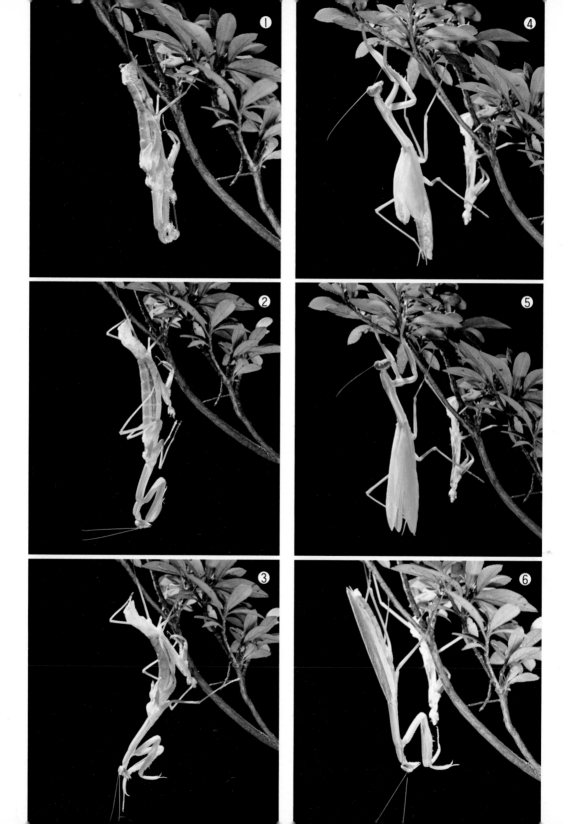

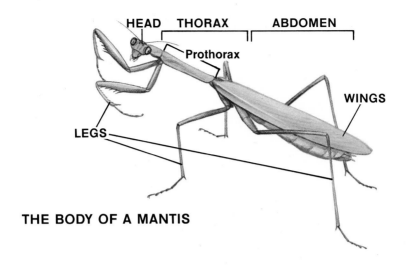

HEAD THORAX ABDOMEN

Prothorax

WINGS

LEGS

THE BODY OF A MANTIS

An adult mantis is without doubt an exotic-looking insect. Its body has the same parts as the bodies of other insects, but they are put together in a very distinctive way.

A mantis's body is divided into three main parts—the head, the thorax, and the abdomen. On the head are located the insect's eyes, its mouth, and two long, thin **antennae,** sense organs used to smell and feel. The mantis's four wings and six legs are attached to the thorax, the middle section of the body. The abdomen is the last section of the body, containing the organs of digestion and reproduction.

It is the form of its thorax that gives the mantis its unique appearance. Compared to the thoraxes of other insects, it is extremely elongated. The **prothorax**—the first section of the thorax, to which the front legs are attached—is particularly long and thin. It is also very flexible, turning and bending easily.

These features not only contribute to the mantis's unique appearance but also play a part in its skill as a hunter.

Left: This multiple-exposure photograph shows how easily a mantis can turn its head and upper body. *Opposite:* A mantis hunting by moonlight. Its front legs are raised in the "praying" position that has given the insect one of its common names.

Hunting is one of the main occupations of an adult mantis. Unlike many other short-lived insects, it has an active adult lifespan of several months, and it needs plenty of food during this time.

The mantis is a stealthy hunter, lying in wait for its prey instead of pursuing it actively. Perched on a tree or bush, the insect sits with its head erect and "praying arms" raised, alert to the approach of a potential meal. Its large eyes watch the surrounding territory, while its sensitive antennae respond to odors and vibrations in the air.

The flexibility of a mantis's body enables the insect to keep an eye on what is happening all around its perch. Its head as well as its prothorax can be twisted and turned easily. In fact, the mantis is one of the few insects capable of moving its head from side to side and up and down. It is an ability that is very useful to this patient hunter.

The pictures on these two pages show what happens when a butterfly comes too close to a hunting mantis. In a blur of movement, the mantis reaches out with its powerful front legs and seizes the insect before it has a chance to escape.

This pair of deadly legs is another unusual physical feature that makes the mantis a skillful hunter. The insect's front legs are very different from its other two pairs of legs and from the front legs of most other insects.

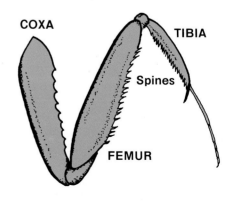

COXA   TIBIA

Spines

FEMUR

The legs of most insects are divided into five major sections or segments, the most important of which are the **coxa,** the **femur,** and the **tibia.** A mantis's front legs have these same sections, but they have been specially modified for seizing and holding prey.

When a mantis seizes a butterfly or some other prey, it holds the insect between the femur and the tibia of one or both front legs. Powerful flexing muscles pull these two segments of the leg together something like the sections of a pocket knife. Rows of sharp spines on the femur and the tibia hold the prey's body in an almost unbreakable grip. Grasping its meal in this way, the mantis uses its strong mouthparts to devour it, usually while the insect is still alive.

A mantis nymph captures a night-flying moth.

The mantis owes some part of its hunting skill to its keen eyesight. The insect's bulging eyes provide good vision both in daylight and during the dark hours of the night.

Like most insects, a mantis has two **compound eyes,** each one made up of hundreds of tiny lenses. The separate images reflected by these lenses combine to produce a kind of mosaic picture of the mantis's surroundings. In addition to its compound eyes, a mantis has three **simple eyes**

In daylight, a mantis's eyes are usually light green or tan (left), but when night falls, they turn dark brown (right).

located between its antennae. (You can see these three eyes clearly in the photograph on the cover of this book.) The simple eyes do not form images but can probably tell the difference between light and dark.

When night falls, a mantis's compound eyes respond to the changes in light by changing color. The pigment, or coloring material, in the normally green or tan eyes becomes dark brown in many species. Because it is able to absorb more of the available light, the dark pigment increases the sensitivity of the mantis's eyes and improves its vision for night hunting.

Opposite: A mantis captures a grasshopper. *Right:* After eating, a mantis cleans its front legs with its mouthparts.

Day or night, the mantis is a tireless predator, constantly on the watch for moths, butterflies, grasshoppers, and other insects to feed its enormous appetite. Large species of mantises may even attack small frogs, lizards, and birds in their never-ending search for food.

Mantises may be voracious predators, but they have very tidy eating habits. After a mantis finishes a meal, it carefully cleans its front legs by nibbling on them with its **mandibles,** or jaws. It may also pull its antennae down and give them a cleaning as well.

A mantis caught in a spider web

Sometimes mantises find themselves playing the role of prey rather than predator. Adult mantises have few natural enemies in the insect world, but other kinds of animals hunt and eat them. Birds, lizards, and some small mammals prey on mantises. Mantises in flight sometimes blunder into spider webs and become trapped by the sticky silk thread. Then they end up as meals for the resident spiders.

Mantises usually take flight only to move from one perch to another or to escape from predators. They are not long-distance fliers. Adult female mantises are often incapable of flight because their bodies are heavy with the weight of undeveloped eggs.

Opposite: **A pair of mantises mating. The smaller male is on top of the female.**

Autumn is the time of mating for mantises in temperate climates. The large females, their bodies swollen with eggs, are sought out eagerly by the smaller, slimmer males. The male mantises, however, must be cautious in approaching potential partners, or they will end up as meals rather than mates. Any mantis will eat another mantis if it gets a chance, and mating females are no exception to this rule.

A male usually approaches a female from behind and climbs onto her back, holding on with his front legs. Then he bends the tip of his abdomen under to join the tip of the female's abdomen. Sperm cells pass from the male's body to the female's, where they are stored in a special chamber in her abdomen.

Even after a male mantis has mated with a female, he is not safe from her tremendous appetite. Females often seize their partners and devour them as soon as they have finished mating. In fact, they sometimes attack the males during the mating act. Males do not resist these attacks and even try to finish their tasks before they are eaten by their ferocious mates.

Left: A female mantis attacking her partner after mating. *Opposite:* A female devouring a wasp. Females need nourishment to prepare themselves for the job of egg laying.

If a male mantis survives mating, he may live for a few weeks longer, but the coming of cold weather will soon bring an end to the natural cycle of his life. His mate's life will also end with the coming of winter, but the female mantis has a big job to do before she dies.

For a few days after mating, the female hunts as usual, seeking nourishing food to strengthen her for the work ahead. Then she stops her activities and takes up a position on a tree branch or sturdy twig. The time has come to lay her eggs.

40

Opposite: A female releases the material that forms the egg case. *Right:* The mantis uses the tip of her abdomen to whip the material into a foamy mass.

The female mantis begins the egg-laying process by making the ootheca, or egg case, that will shelter the eggs. Clinging head downward to her chosen twig, she releases a frothy material from glands located in her abdomen. The mantis whips this material into a foamy mass with circular movements of the tip of her abdomen.

Into the center of the soft egg case, the female deposits her eggs. As each egg passes through her reproductive system, it is united with a male sperm cell. The eggs leave the female's body through the **ovipositor,** a kind of tube at the end of her abdomen.

Using her ovipositor, the female shapes the foamy material of the egg case into tiny chambers that hold the eggs. Each chamber is connected to the outside of the case by a narrow passageway through which the mantis nymph will eventually emerge. It takes about three hours for the female to build this complicated structure, and she does it completely by instinct, without even looking at her handiwork.

The natural lifespan of an adult mantis ends in late autumn, when the dry leaves fall from the trees.

Some female mantises build only one large egg case, containing as many as 400 eggs. Females of other species construct several smaller cases that hold fewer eggs.

About an hour after an egg case is completed, its surface becomes hard and leathery. This tough exterior will protect the case from wind, rain, and snow. Inside the case, the spongy material surrounding the eggs is filled with air bubbles that provide insulation against cold.

Protected in this way, the mantis eggs will survive the harsh winter weather. When spring arrives, the eggs will develop into a new generation of mantises that will wiggle out of the case, ready to begin their careers as fearless and skillful hunters.

44

GLOSSARY

antennae (an-TEN-ee) — sense organs on the heads of insects that respond to vibrations and odors

compound eyes — insect eyes made up of many tiny lenses and capable of seeing images and colors

coxa (KAHK-seh) — one of the main sections of an insect's leg

egg cases — the hard capsules that protect mantis eggs during the winter. Female mantises make the cases out of a foamy material produced inside their bodies.

exoskeleton — the tough outer covering of an insect's body that protects the internal organs and provides a framework for muscles

femur (FEE-mur) — one of the main sections of an insect's leg

mandibles (MAN-dih-b'ls) — insect jaws used to hold and chew food

Mantodea (man-toe-DEE-uh) — the scientific order in which some scientists place mantises. Other scientists consider the insects to be members of the order Orthoptera.

metamorphosis (met-uh-MOR-fuh-sis) — the process of growth and change that produces most adult insects. Mantises, grasshoppers, crickets, dragonflies, and a few other insects go through a gradual three-stage development known as **incomplete metamorphosis**; the three stages are egg, nymph, and adult. **Complete metamorphosis** has four stages: egg, larva, pupa, and adult. Bees, butterflies, ants, and many other kinds of insects develop by this process.

molt — to shed the outer covering of the body

nymph (NIMF)—the immature form of mantises and other insects that develop through incomplete metamorphosis

oothecae (oo-THEE-kee)—the egg cases made by female mantises. The singular form of the word is **ootheca**, pronounced oo-THEE-kuh.

Orthoptera (or-THOP-teh-ruh)—the scientific order to which grasshoppers, crickets, and cockroaches belong. Some scientists place mantises in this order.

ovipositor (oh-vee-POS-ih-tur)—a tube at the end of a female insect's abdomen through which eggs leave the body

predators—animals that hunt and kill other animals for food

prey—an animal killed by another animal and used for food

prothorax—the first section of an insect's thorax, to which the front legs are attached

simple eyes—insect eyes each made up of a single lens and able to tell the difference between dark and light

species (SPEE-shees)—a group of animals that have many characteristics in common. Species is the basic unit in the system of scientific classification.

tibia (TIB-ee-uh)—one of the main sections of an insect's leg

thorax (THOR-aks)—the middle section of an insect's body

wing pads—small pads of tissue on a nymph's thorax that develop into the wings of the adult mantis

INDEX